Blood & Ink

Verses and Words For The Rebel Soul

PAMELA IBARRA

BookLeaf Publishing

India | USA | UK

To Mikey, my beautiful, amazing, and inspiring boy, you never cease to amaze me. I see my reflection in you. I can not be more grateful for my friends, family, and loved ones.

This book is dedicated to my family, who have been my anchor and light. Mikey, your innocence and laughter inspire me to see the world with wonder and hope. I am thankful for the Universe, which allowed me to meet amazing and inspiring people on my journey.

While writing these poems, I was able to express my chaos and darkness and fully embrace my duality. Through every shadow and every spark of light, you have shown me the beauty of being human.

Finally, this book is for anyone seeking healing, self-awareness, and the courage to decolonize their soul. May these poems guide you as they have guided me.

Acknowledgments

The existence of this book is based on my perseverance. Against all odds, doubts, and fears, I took a chance on myself because of my unshakable resolve to find and use my voice, even when no one was listening. I found freedom when I expressed myself through my writing. For that, I begin by honoring my journey through darkness, growth, and light, embracing the duality within me.

Thank you to those who have stood beside me, unwavering in their love and belief. To my family, who may not always understand my path but still choose to walk beside me, I love you for your patience and presence.

To my closest friends, the ones who saw the tears behind my verses and still encouraged me to share them: you are my chosen family, my safety nets, my muses. Your faith in my voice gave me the courage to create.

To the poets and thinkers who inspired me—living, gone, or unnamed—I owe you my gratitude for showing me that words can be weapons, medicine, and bridges to connection.

To the unseen moments of turmoil and chaos, I am thankful that I transformed those moments into something raw and real, a testament to the transformative power of art. Finally, to you, the reader, who saw something in this book and is now holding it in your hands: thank you for listening. These words are mine, but they are also yours. May they serve as a mirror, a spark, or a companion on your path. I hope they resonate with you and bring you comfort or inspiration.

With all my heart,

Pamela Ibarra

Preface

With poetry, I have been able to express those haunting and consuming thoughts with ink, rationalize my emotions, and find my voice. I transformed and alchemized my inner demons and my emotions to forge this weapon through the landscapes of my heart and mind. Chaos, madness, hope, and resilience. In my own world, I will forever be the warrior, the fighter, and the poet. With quiet introspection and fiery emotion, these verses reflect my attempt to make sense of a complex world and inspire transformation in others.

Each poem recalls my ideals, values, emotions, and thoughts caught in the net of language. Together, they weave a narrative that is at once personal and universal—a tapestry of emotions and experiences that connect us all, reminding us of our shared humanity.

I invite you into my inner world through these pages while encouraging you to reflect.

Thank you for allowing me to share this journey with you.

— Pamela Ibarra

What is Humanity?

Humanity has lost its meaning.
Humankind is no longer human,
Humans are no longer kind.
We have turned into beasts,
Rebels and scavengers,
Fighting on instinct,
Without a vision.
We've lost our mission.
No morality,

No integrity,
Without individuality,
No creativity or knowledge.
We have forsaken our values
For a couple of dollars.
How sad it is to realize what we've become—
A life without empathy
For our sister,
For our brother.
A civilization with no tomorrow,
A tribe of imbeciles
Amid the rubble of our despair.
But never forget:
Humankind has the mindset and the power
To be whatever we aspire to be.
Let us not turn into creatures of greed and
arrogance,
Of superiority, intolerance, and madness.
Rise above.
For the future is now,
And tomorrow will not wait
For humanity to learn its lesson.

Delaying the Inevitable

Delaying the inevitable
is denying yourself
the opportunity to grow and evolve
into the best version of yourself.
I am divinely and spiritually protected.
I walk with the strength of my ancestors,
the righteous rage of the divine feminine,
the courage of the masculine energy of
victorious warriors,

and the sacred wisdom of my elders.
The wind carries their voices.
The fire holds their warmth.
The water reflects the clarity of their souls.
The earth cradles the roots—
the foundation of our destiny.
My destiny.
The moon shines down,
whispering secrets of resilience.
The sun caresses my cheeks with joy,
a sign of encouragement and hope.
Succumb willingly
to the divine intervention of time
and its magical illusions.
Delaying the inevitable
is denying yourself
the opportunity to grow and evolve
into the best version of yourself.
Delaying the inevitable
is denying your path.

Purity and Venom

It was all clear...
When I had disappeared—
Deep, deep into my madness.
Was I buried alive in my own conscience?
Like a puppet to its master,
I obeyed the strings of laughter.
Keep pretending... like a daydream.
Clear like water, cold like snow—
It's what my reflection shows.
Don't let the venom consume me.
I'm drowning in the poison,
Hanging in the abyss.
Keep on smiling... keep on crying,

While my purity is stripped from me.
Crystal tears, floating in despair.
The venom of this madness—
I can feel it in the air.
I can savor salty teardrops.
I can feel my soul die slowly.
My heart aches in pain;
My screams are in vain.
Don't surrender to my mind,
Though my body is growing numb.
It was all clear…
I had disappeared—
Deep, deep into my mind,
Burying my thoughts of anger and sadness.
Like a puppet, like a toy,
I had no use for your joy.
And my dignity? No more.
Weakness overpowered me.
All it took was a drop of venom—
From your evil—to consume me.
For my purity is no more.
Another false illusion.
And you…
You will be a shadow lurking in my mind,
A haunting presence for all time.

Puddle of Mud

Follow me through the darkness,
Get away from the roaches
That play in a puddle of mud.
I am filled with hate and anger.
In the world, nobody seems good to me.
I'm alone with myself.
Follow me through the darkness.
So you can see the light,
See what's real.

Stupid society still doesn't see reality.
Stupid humanity still believes in fantasy.
My nightmares drag you into my darkest
coven,
And myself.
I wish they were true,
So you could see what I feel,
See what I see.
I won't be fooled by what you think.
Does your mind even think?
Your words, unspoken, better be.
Follow me through the darkness,
Get away from the roaches
That play in a puddle of mud.

I Understood Clearly

The meaning...
The purpose...
The journey...
Words of madness,
Chaos, thoughts, and visions
Floating...
Roaming...
Materializing in thin air...
The time is changing,

Shifting slowly...
Words of sadness,
Pain, sorrow, and blindness...
Flowing...
Rolling...
Streaming down my eyes...
It's no use...
The desire to feel nothing,
And the curse of feeling all so profoundly...
The paradox of life and death—
My blessing and my curse.

Blank

My mind is now blank,
I am running out of ink
To write sweet words,
A symphony.
I am running out of love;
All the feelings that I felt
Are no longer here
They disappeared
I guess they melt,

Like ice cream on a hot, hot day.
I am running out of fucks to give—
It never meant a single thing.
I used to be so sweet and subtle,
But why do I even bother?
I am running out of life.
It passes me slowly, and I cannot hide.

Daughter of The Moon

Not everyone can feel like sunshine—
Warm, loving, and kind.
Rainbows and butterflies,
Gentle and soft.
Some of us are the reflection of your
sunshine.
We are the moon,
Showing you reality,
Breaking through the illusion

Of the consciousness of mankind.
We are appreciated during the dark times,
But we are not celebrated.
We are comfort,
But we are also truth.
And truth sometimes hurts.
We are kind but not always nice.
I know I don't come in and light up the room,
But I am that space
For you to show your darkness.
Because, like the moon,
I'm not scared of the dark.
I can be the moonlight
Until you find your sunshine again.

She Belonged to Herself

She carried and embraced the depth of her
spirit with such grace,
Balancing her light and her darkness
effortlessly.
Both the heavens and the underworld fought
over her soul,
Desperate to obtain control.
But she belonged to no one;
She belonged nowhere—
Only to herself and herself alone.
She had the heart of a poet,

Writing her destiny in the firmament with
stardust,
Dipping her pen in the ink of the silver moon.
She had the courage of a warrior,
Battling each day,
Fighting against time.
The essence of an artist,
Painting the canvas of her reality.
The voice of a siren,
Luring you down into the depths of her soul.
The power of a beast,
Always waiting to attack.
The mind of a ruler,
Strategically studying her enemies,
With a strong sense of justice.
She carried the sacred rage of her ancestors,
Prideful and unwavering,
A badge of honor etched in her being.
She belonged to her own world—
Her own time,
Her own rules,
Her own life.
And though she was all over the place,
It was she who called it home.

Destiny, oh destiny

Tides of time crashing by,
Washing away my doubts, my faults.
Waves of emotional turmoil,
Slowly consuming me, embracing me,
Cover me gently... nostalgia, memories...
Tides of time wash over me, cleanse me,
Purify me—baptized by divine intervention.
The ultimate creation, renewal, salvation.
In the quiet whisper of dawn's embrace,

I feel the tides of time, a gentle grace.
Each wave that crashes, each surge that flows,
Carries away the weight of woes.
Memories dance in the moonlit sea,
Echoes of what was, what is, what will be.
In this eternal ebb and flow,
Destiny's path begins to show.
Through storms and calm, through highs and
lows,
A journey unfolds as the river flows.
In the tides of time, I find my way,
Guided by stars through night and day.
Embraced by waves, both fierce and kind,
I surrender to the currents and leave fear
behind.
In this vast ocean of fate's design,
I am renewed—I touch the divine.
Tides of time carry me to the shores of the
unknown,
Where destiny awaits, where seeds are sown.
In the dance of waves, in the rhythm of the
sea,
I find my place; I find my destiny.

Embrace Of Darkness

In the darkness, I find comfort and
consolation,
A place to speak through madness and chaos.
Rage consumes my words,
Spitting fire and venom—
A beast has awakened.
Pain, hurt, and terror ignite within me,
Ready to attack.
My voice is a weapon of war,

My words are swords,
Sharpened for battles of truth—
A bloodbath of unheard tales,
Each one soaked in sorrow.
I sharpen my tongue,
Harmonizing to the beat of war drums.
The sound of destiny calls upon me,
And I answer with pride.

Who Are You?

Who are you?

You ask me.

I'm a beast, not to be tamed,

A winged demon, not to be named.

I am the creator and the destructor,

A reflector and a distractor.

Who are you?

You ask again.

I'm a creature with fangs, claws, and fire,

Not made to fit your deepest desire.
I'm a shadow that lingers, searching for prey,
Collecting the souls of those who must pay.
I'm the dragon that lives within—
Unseen, untamed, alive beneath the skin

I Am Karma

Devotion to me,
I know you seek.
I am karma, you see,
The contemplation, the admiration,
Of a new empire yet to begin—
The adoration is all for me.
I have the power to take,
The power to give,
To punish or reward as I please.

Is it mercy? Is it defeat?
Balancing the scales of light and dark,
To find the perfect shade of grey
On this insane, lonely day.
My judgment isn't clouded by silly little
fantasies;
It's ruled by the severity of this complex
reality.
The spectacle! The show!
Am I the main character?
I am karma, you see.
Come to me, and you will see—
Where will the path to your destiny lead?
Devotion to me,
I know you seek.
I am karma, you see,
The contemplation, the admiration,
Of a new empire yet to begin—
The adoration is all for me.
And now your soul belongs to me.
I guess karma really is a bitch.

We are humans

We are humans.
Complex and fragile creatures,
Monsters and demons
In other people's stories—
At times, even villains.
We are angels, divine beings,
Heroes basking in our own glory,
Celebrating victories—
Oh, those bittersweet memories—

While others crumble in silent defeat.
We were born "free,"
Yet bound by the freedom to obey
The circumstances of our environment.
We are magic and logic,
Intertwined,
An illusion we create
To build our reality,
To shield ourselves from our own fragility.
We are humans.
Flesh and bone,
Dressed in false morals—
An unethical attire,
Tailored to endless desire.
We are humans.
Meant to become what we must
To coexist,
To believe what we need to believe.

Welcome to the Hell You Created

I hope the flames of the hell you created
Reach you, and burn with the intensity
You wished for others.
May you feel the scorch ten times over.
May they swallow you whole, consume you,
For the pain you wished, inflicted, and
ignored.

I wish it back upon you—
To incinerate your very soul.
Fighting fire with fire,
Till the end,
Until there is nothing left to burn.
That may be the only way we will learn.
Welcome to the hell you created.

Divine Feminine

With your hair down,
Covered in stardust and the mist of pure
wind,
Let it weigh you down like a blanket of
protection
For your insecurities.
With your hair up,
Standing in confidence—
No need to hide anymore,
Don't conceal your beauty and grace.
You are worthy.
You are loved, protected, and divine.

Divine Feminine...
Crone and wise,
Bold and fierce,
Fire in your soul, fire in your eyes.
Water to extinguish the flames of infernal
rage,
To cleanse the spirit when it tires.
Earth to keep you grounded,
Air to keep you flying.
Don't surrender to life,
Divine Feminine.
Life forms within our vessels,
In our rituals of blood.
In the pain, we find our power.
You fucked up—
You only made us stronger.
We are worthy, loved, protected—we are
divine.
The rise of the phoenix, to create,
Sometimes, we must destroy.
Burn it all down, then build it all up.
Divine Feminine,
I will wait a little longer.
We will rise to power and take what is ours.

To Be...

They sold me a lie—
An expensive one.
An expensive life.
As if that weren't enough,
I feel cheated.
In turmoil—my identity, my fucking
humanity.
Don't you see the insanity?
This existence—questioned, diminished,
By double standards of fake morality.

I feel cheated in this life,
In this time, in this world.
It's cruel to exist—just to please.
Cheated, robbed, violated, hurt.
I feel unworthy and in pain.
Less than yesterday,
Less again tomorrow.
My worth—defined by men's opinions,
By institutional religion.
A living contradiction.
A problem to solve.
A sin in the flesh.
Madness swells, swallowing my fear.
Thoughts and emotions, rushing and striking,
Tearing through my body.
I wish I could disappear.
Spare me your sermons, your mediocrity,
Your judgment, your hypocrisy.
I don't want your love, your glorification,
Your hollow honor, your sacrifices.
I don't need your celebrations.
Respect—
That is all I want.
Respect—
That is all I need

Toxic

I guess I was hallucinating,
As I stared back at my reflection.
Toxicity reflected onto others,
The colors bouncing off my body—
A spectrum of shadows and power.
I was toxic.
Like raindrops and light creating a rainbow,
I delivered my anger with surgical precision.
Trapped inside my own prison,
A mirror reflecting only hatred.
It didn't matter who I affected;
I lingered in my misery,
Floating in despair,
Grasping for new air

Your Salvation

Delicate fragments of my essence
Wandered, searching for your presence.
I savored every flavor of your form—
A vessel of lust to hold and transform.
I devoured the sins you had to offer,
Colliding in whispers of divine slaughter.
Surrendered to temptation's sweet decree,
An altar of adoration I built for thee.
For your name, I cry in desperation,
I kneel in awe, my complete submission.
Proclaiming your name, oh goddess divine,
For your salvation is forever mine.

A Weapon of Truth

The most powerful weapon
that humanity possesses
is a word that's been spoken.
It can transmit emotions—
happiness or sadness,
start or end a war,
break a heart or mend a soul.
A word, born as an idea,
follows the action to become a plan,

a goal, a lifestyle, a reality.
Speak your truth—and believe it.
It's a balance
between harmony and agony.
A word of kindness or a word of madness—
The choice is yours.
For being human is no crime,
and there is no good or evil—
only a choice, only a decision.
Unload your gun.
Put down the knife.
Keep up the act, if you must—
but what difference will it make?
What will this act create?
How about silence?
How about peace?
Keep your mouth shut.
Be quiet and be kind.
Not everyone needs to know
what you think all the time.
For a person with peace
in mind and soul
is in peace with the world—
and leaves the world alone.

A Day

Give me a day with a sinner
to hear their tales of becoming a winner.
To taste power—
to devour another's happiness
and rip their humanity and soul apart.
Give me a day with a sinner
to learn the atrocities of our society.
Give me a day without empathy,
a day of blissful ignorance,
to walk around like a zombie.
Give me a day with a villain
to learn their religion—
and show them I am their competition.

Untamed

I don't bow.
I don't beg.
I don't submit.
I won't surrender.
I own myself—
and nobody else.
No religion, no institution,
no person, no law governs me.
I write my own rules.
I know my limits.
I refuse to abide
by society's expectations.

Universe

There is a universe in your mind,
Always in control, all the time.
There's lightning, there's thunder
When you laugh or when you struggle.
A river of tears begins to flow
When you're sad or gripped by fear.
There are constellations in your gaze;
I see the moon and the stars all day.
Your body's scent is like fresh blooms,
Blossoming in the heart of spring.
And your hair cascades like the night—dark,
Encircling all that is bright.

Waiting For The End

I walked beneath the moonlight,
Soaking in its silvery glow,
Blending into the darkness.
Waiting...
I was waiting for a sign,
A sign from the divine,
A signal to survive.
Waiting...
The stars became my guides—

My protectors, my mentors.
My spirit elevated, soaring toward the sky.
Waiting...
A voice within me whispered:
How will you survive?
Terrified and weak,
I kept walking in defeat.
Waiting...
Then, I stopped and realized
The answer lay within:
I was born a survivor—no need to fantasize
Only I could save myself from the cold, from
this world.
I was my own savior.
Through every pain I endured,
I was the one
Who listened to my cries,
The one who gathered the shards of my
broken heart.
No more waiting or wasting time.
It's time to rise—be your own savior.
The night embraced me, eased my fear,
It helped me heal, and I was saved as I closed
my eyes.

Don't Give Up

You've tasted your own blood from the pain
You've emptied bottle after bottles
And have drowned in them your sorrows
You've reached out again and again
For help and not complain
You're sinking deeper into the abyss of your
hell
Spinning round and round like a carousel
You are suffocating with every word you
speak

But all you hear is your own shriek
Your shattered soul is no longer whole
Emptiness has covered all
And the present is no gift
And you wish you didn't exist
And you wish for fewer days
And your faith starts to decay
Rotting in a funeral grave
But your body is alive
And your future is still bright
Don't give up
You are here to shine

Dreamer

I may be a dreamer
Cause I live near the clouds,
Out of reach, untouchable,
Yet my feet stay grounded in reality.
I carry the weight of the world in silence,
Speaking only when my thoughts are loud
enough to drown out my fears.
I stare into the abyss,
My eyes burn as I search for meaning
In the darkness that surrounds me.
I whisper to the void,
I hope my voice will echo back with answers I
can never find.

I may not be a winner
But I'll never be a quitter
My failure is not my defeat;
It's the fuel that feeds the fire of my resistance
I keep dreaming,
Keep pushing through the storms,
Determined to make my daydreams real.
I will hold on tight to what's mine,
Even when the winds of doubt try to tear it
away.
I will stand tall,
My soul, a fortress of resolve,
No matter how many times life tries to break
me.
I will survive,
Not just for me but for the dream that keeps
me alive.
Let our lives intertwine,
Not with the fragility of fleeting moments,
But with the strength of bonds that never say
goodbye,
Even when the world falls apart around us.
We will endure,
Because we are the dreamers who refuse to be
forgotten.

Bleed

I bleed liquid gold
As the wounds learn to heal.
All my scars are too real,
With my tears crystal clear,
Making my smile disappear.
I bleed liquid gold, now you see,
Transformed
From human to goddess,
When I woke from my dream,
Reincarnated from ashes.
You killed the old me.
Try to hurt me, you fool.
I will bleed liquid gold.
Now, the pain I can fake,
And your life, I can take

Cycle of Life

Cycle begins,
Breathing,
Suffocating,
Half drowning,
Half flying,
Half surviving,
Half overcoming,
Half living,
Half dying.

My bones showing,
My skin glowing,
My dreams soaring,
My heart breaking,
Ups and downs,
The cycle of my life,
A never-ending rollercoaster of fun,
Reminding me I'm still alive.

Time

Tick... tock...
Time as a hero...
It helps you heal...
One day, those wounds
It will slowly disappear...
As time goes by,
It makes you wise...
To be forgetful of their mistakes...
In the remembrance

Of your own faith...
Tick... tock...
Time as a villain...
It can be cruel...
The desperation...
One day will rule...
For some mistakes cannot be forgotten...
So I'm impatient...
Can't wait for karma
To find its way...
So now it's time for them to pay...
It might be long overdue...
But what an honor to be your doom...
Hope you enjoy your demise...
I'll be in my paradise...

Slay, slay, slay... Slay the beast.

Call the weak...
Conquer the majestic...
Imprison the divine...
Kill, kill, kill...
Slay the monsters and the demons.
We fear the darkness,
We fear what lurks inside—

Inside our minds, our souls,
The voices... the truth.
Destruction is the easier path—
To point fingers,
To judge,
To hate what we fail to comprehend.
We are blinded by the light or lost in the
darkness.
Coexist.
Find middle ground—
Or remain forever unfound.

The inner child in me is begging for salvation.

The weight of life consumes me to my core...
I had to choose better...
I can't believe in anything anymore...
Only me... yet I remain.
*"It's time to comfort my inner child—time to
embrace my shadow self."*
*"You did all you could to survive
In this cruel, unrelenting world."*

Mind Trap

Self-sabotage is real... imposter syndrome is
real...
At times, I want to give up on everything,
But my stubbornness—my masochistic
tendencies—won't let me quit.
Why can't I be a quitter?
Why can't I just not care?
Even when you have faced your demons...
You confront them, befriend them, or tame

them.
And after that, you still have to face the ugly
truths
Of this cruel, unforgiving world.
Am I REALLY stepping away from this
infernal nightmare
Only to walk into another HELL?
Then, you dissociate and revert to survival
mode.
Survive.
Let me just survive...
Anxiety worsens day by day,
Sadness drips away, piece by piece...
The real you, hiding behind fake masks,
Faking that everything is alright.
Self-sabotage creeps in... imposter syndrome
lingers...
Wishing every day to surpass this feeling—it's
surreal.
I'm just getting tired of being trapped in my
mind.

HOME

I was meant to walk through the darkness,
To surrender to the embrace of the night,
To sit upon the throne of bloody thorns.
I was destined for chaos, to thrive in despair.
Why fight the inevitable?
Why resist the creeping dread?
Why battle the everlasting gloom?
I belong to the darkness; I belong to my
shadows.
I whisper as
We hold hands again,
Nowhere to hide, nowhere to run from
myself.
It is time to go home.

In my sleep

I was lost, deep within my soul.
I was lost...
I hid all the ugly parts of me,
They surfaced later...
In my defense,
My shadow self endured endless pain and
suffering.
It was just an everyday game,
A game I was forced to play...
I was hiding in the shadows,
Scared and alone.
I dwelled in darkness, lost in my thoughts,
With only my demons to keep me company.
I despised myself for accepting humiliation...

"The world owes you nothing, but you owe everything to the world." — Pam.

"The greatest victory is one that requires no battle. Thought and balance bring success. Upright and honest rule the day."— Pam

"You can't accept the bare minimum from the extraordinary, and you can't expect the extraordinary from those who do the bare minimum. Mediocrity does not align with your purpose."— Pam.

9 789369 543441